Letters of

A THOUSAND SPEECHES

Titles
by S. Sulianah

Masterpiece in Your Heart – A Series of Poetry

Letters of
A THOUSAND SPEECHES

WINTER SCRIBBLER™
Publishing

Winter Scribbler Publishing
Singapore
Business Registration No. 53339284E
www.winterscribbler.com

Author S.Sulianah
www.ctsulianah.com

Cover Design Ikrima Art Studio
Illustrations Sigit Gilal

National Library Board, Singapore Cataloguing in Publication Data
Name(s): S. Sulianah.
Title: Letters of a thousand speeches : prose poetry / S. Sulianah.
Description: Singapore : Winter Scribbler Publishing, [2020]
Identifier(s): OCN 1223307667 | ISBN 978-981-14-8971-6 (paperback)
Subject(s): LCSH: Love poetry.
Classification: DDC S821--dc23

Introduction

When I told you I could write hundreds of letters filled with a thousand speeches, what I meant was I have done it since the day we met again seven years ago.

Your kindness, attention, protectiveness, wit and curiosity have lit up my life. Every time you smile, it seeps into my mind, begging to be in my memory.

The way you laughed and how you hid that beautiful shy smile puts me to sleep at night.

I thought I had lost all this seven years ago. And then you came back.

Remember when both of us were asking each other, whether poems are inspired when we are sad or when we have everything in our lives?

I knew what it was, but I had no courage to tell you.

That one muse.

Have you ever wondered
how a person can fill
every single page—

beautifying each breath
filled with words of longing,
pining for affection,
embossing the empty soul
by being this bold?

Ten, eleven or even twenty-two years ago, I do not feel this way. Probably, someone else was filling that space.

You were as beautiful as you once were.

I have yet to find the reason that we have been brought together after decades, when we both know we have nothing in common.

C
C
C
C
C
Bb
F
F
F
F
F
G
G
G
G
G
A
A
A
A

C C F G A
C F G A
C G F G A F
C G C F G-A-G F
Bb F A F G F

the musical carousel

April 20, 2013

In the beginning, I could feel myself engulfed with notes of worry and fear.

When I saw you again with all of our friends after years, my heart tried to tell me that you are the one who will fill this empty space. I could feel that when I looked into your eyes and when we hugged.

I was trying to warm myself by not looking into those lingering beautiful eyes of yours, piercing through the walls that I have built over the years.

till five

April 22, 2013

Every time you asked me out, my nerves were out of tune with the beat of my heart. I anticipated every moment I could hold onto. I will try to remember your laugh and voice so that I will not crave it at the end of the night.

I can repeat the jokes you made, making sure you know that I listened to every bit of it. Laughing casually, I hid my fluttering heart.

I always find your sweet smiles genuine. I have seen hundreds of dimples, but I did not anticipate that yours could make me steal glances whenever you look away.

Those perfectly shaped lips of yours make my mind imagine its tenderness.

I look forward to those moments of intentional touches and stealing glances.

At the end of the night when we bid each other goodbye, the scent of your perfume and the flashbacks keeps me awake till early morning.

And, I told you I like you more than a friend.

April 25, 2013

I know you could hold onto that fear. There is nothing frightening in the scene of the movie. Yet, you decided to scream at the end and hugged me.

The only moments I remember about this movie are how bland it was, the moment when our fingers held onto each other's, and how I could not stop thinking about you when you were right beside me.

April 27, 2013

I have no control over how this happens.
Now, you are the one who stays in my mind,

stealing my daydreams with all the what ifs.
You are the comfort to the coldness of my nights.

Could you see through me?

Did I tell you too much with my glance and graces?

Do you have any idea that you already have a special place in my heart?

miss me... miss you
May 16, 2013

Rays of sunshine saturate the dusk.

Your text said that you missed my nonsense,
while here I am missing you too.

This awkward want burns my days
and weird, unexplainable flashbacks of you fill my nights.

I hope you do something about this.

I am worried that I will hurt the deep part of my being. Rather than enduring the possibilities of getting my heart hurt, I will not make any first step towards you. I will leave everything let you be with the person you are in love with.

fears

May 17, 2013

These unknown ticks of assumption and worry are back in place again. Wild guesses start to haunt my mind.

I keep asking myself the reasons for this overwhelming uncertainty. Whenever these moments cloud my unclear mind, my immediate decision is to let you go.

You have the right to be with anyone.

How can I go on with this relationship if this fear never leaves?

full moonlit night

May 25, 2013

You were driving.
The moon proudly lit up the roads ahead of us.

It seems like you were in awe of its glorious light, loving every ray embellishing the night sky.

We were engulfed in our own thoughts, while I took those seconds to look into your dark brown orbs. Flashing stories that I have yet to understand.

My wild guesses were that of your love ones. Those who have been part of your life and those who soon will be part of you.

All the while, I was on the other side imagining the things I could do with you.

Travelling to places where none of our friends will know where we are. We will have our morning coffees and dinners. We could do everything without worrying of the don'ts and can'ts.

Where the moon will be with us—
lighting up our hearts and nights.

yellow motorbike

June 23, 2013

I have never stood still staring at someone else like how I did yesterday with you. You were on your motorbike, riding in the lot, passing among the others, making your gorgeous self known to everyone.

I was speechless. My heart stopped beating.

I could not stop smiling the whole time since you arrived. Surprisingly, my brain and the blood pumping to my heart could still function the whole time my eyes were fixated on you.

You never stopped smiling after you got off from your bike with grace. When you walked toward us, I had to stop holding my breath to revive my whole being again.

That beautiful, dimpled smile of yours. You looked so beautiful under the dim streetlight. Charming and stunning. That smile that could probably warm anyone from the cold winter.

Our lingering looks, fixating our eyes on each other. It nearly made me forget about your friend who was beside me all that time.

That intense air between you and me could tune up the soundtrack of those bland films, illustrating musical notes of longing and anticipation.

secret

June 23, 2013

Sometimes, moments or feelings are meant to be kept forever.

Anything could turn out to have negative consequences that could involve losing this friendship.

My solutions to these moments were to avoid meeting you as often as we had been for the past few months. I could tell you what I feel with specifics, but my worry of eventually being rejected and avoided by you made me think of it many times.

I have no idea what I am expecting from you when I am not sure about myself.

avoiding you
June 23, 2013

There are moments when I had decided to leave, ignoring my desire to be with you. Especially when you mentioned your former boyfriend. You said you still love him and could not forget him.

And that is when my heart ticked, "That is it". I have to stop myself from feeling like this when you don't.

Then, when you asked me for your bike key, I told you to say something nice. With that same smile, you said, "I love you".

But I know that is just love like a friend should have.

I passed the bike key to you so that you had to hold my hand and fingers. Instead of holding you, I let you go.

I am so afraid I could feel more than this if I had held onto you longer. Too deep into whatever this is—you hooked me forever.

You kissed me before I boarded the cab.
And that was the first time I was terrified.

I keep reminding myself since this morning to avoid messaging you as usual. This is what happened when fears rules. The only solution I know is avoidance.

I have been telling myself to let nature take its course, especially since you told me that you still love him. This means there is nothing between us.

My heart holds the reins
All this while pulling the strings
She is the master of the ring

breathless

June 26, 2013

What is it like to be kissed by you?

If you could see right through my soul,
she would tell you that every time
I think of you, I couldn't breathe.

mind is you
June 30, 2013

My mind could wander any time during the day.
You are the thief of my time.

You stole every minute of my attention and every second of my carelessness. And whatever you had taken are the most precious to me.

I could not blame you.

You appeared at the right time, a time when my life needed another soul. Another soul to motivate me, to move on with my goals, to forget feelings that have been with me for the last two years.

You made me forget someone who has been in my mind recently.

meaningless songs

June 30, 2013

I can still remember the touch of your soft cheeks, the grace of your arms and fingers on mine.

My mind is filled with the image of you and me together when we were alone.

Everything seems to be muted. The images of the people around us, those guys at the corner of the bar, and the whispers.

I always hear the songs that marked our moments together. "Locked Me Out of Heaven", "When I Was Your Man" and "Just the Way You Are" used to be meaningless to me.

I wish I could ask you whether you feel the same way.

There are no messages from you since that day.
I was the one who initiated it. And when you
did not respond to the recent,
my heart thuds "Stop".

colourful clouds
July 2, 2013

That whisk of noon clouds
Sun shines on the greens

Another reason
to think of you

every single second
July 2, 2013

I have been thinking of you.

Your presence filled my soul,
filling the vacant space in this café.

I did not hear from you for days,
which is unusual.
I am so afraid now that you will
leave without saying goodbye.

Your glowing spirit
glimmering each second,
even during my busy days
and dull nights.

the message of I miss you

July 17, 2013

Contemplating
for a second
to each minute.

Finally,
I did it.

I told you
"I think I miss you".

Then I kept thinking,
did I make a mistake?

You did not respond
from seconds to minutes,
minutes to hours.

Then I realised how stupid I was.

A few hours later,
you replied with a laugh.

At that moment I told myself to stop.
Though you made my days brighter those days,
I can now tell myself to stop before it is too late.

the right route

July 21, 2013

You came by my place, and we met on my block for a second time. There has to be a reason why we are back to this.

Every time you speak about being a better person, I feel bad. I know how ruthless I am to imagine being with you when it is not right.

I do not want to be the villain obstructing you from being a better person.

every time

July 23, 2013

Thinking of you every time seems to be the passcode of my day-to-day motivation. I think of what if we are together, sharing everything in our lives with each other.

you

Aug 22, 2013

Every time I meet you, I have countless expressions and ideas to write.

I could write about how beautiful the snow in New York is—when it is only rain that falls from the sky, frozen.

I could write about how I feel when I am with you, comparing it to the breeze and how blissful it is—when it is only the cold wind from the north.

I could write about how my mind wanders every day thinking of you, describing how beautiful it is—when in reality, it hurts my whole being.

yesterday

Aug 22, 2013

Yesterday, you were so beautiful that I could not take my eyes off you. The last time we met was two weeks ago.

I stood and walked so close to you all night. At times, our shoulders grace each other and so do our hands.

I got to do what I have been dreaming of all week. You told me to touch your cheeks and caress your dimples, and we hugged longer than we should have.

How can anyone not fall for those dimples,
deep and so haunting.

I wonder what would happen
if we both let our hearts lead.

31 Aug 2013

I lost my way at the end of the island.
You responded to my Facebook status privately, and we arranged to meet at IKEA.

That afternoon, you drove me and your little boy to your mum's and then to your favourite aunt's.

While at your mum's, we spent some time together with both of them. Then, you took off your black cardigan, revealing your fitted sleeveless shirt. I was behind you by accident staring at your side. Unfamiliar thud started somewhere in my heart. I had never felt the need until that particular moment.

We hang out a number of times with your boy, which makes me feel like I am special to you.

Those days at the drum school and shopping for furniture are some of my favourite moments with you.

I keep telling myself you do not feel the same way that I feel towards you.

Tell me if I am wrong. You seem to move away when I am too close to you. It seems you are uncomfortable when I shift nearer to you to talk or when our faces are inches away from each other.

Initially, I did this intentionally. Flirting to see how you would react until towards the end of the night.

When you started to drift, I could feel you were not there with me.Subtly, I told myself to stop.

You still talked to your friend about your former boyfriend, and then you sat further away from me. I too started to do the same.

At the end of the night, I tried to hold on to your arms, but when you still avoided me, I let go.

Again, I thought this was it.

Today, all the beautiful moments start engulfing my mind, forgetting yesterday. I am persistent not to give up, to at least try.

Why can't we change this?

If you do not feel the same way,
If you feel that I have peculiar feelings
towards you,
why don't you tell me so I can stop?

trying to forget you

November 3, 2013

Trying to forget you is like trying to remove the tattoo on the back of your neck.

I have to force myself to think of someone else, to focus on my goals in life, and to find other missing pieces.

I need to keep reminding myself not to think of you once the sun rises, and not to need being with you when the night comes.

And then few days later,
I came back to the same old play again.

doubts and throbs

December 5, 2013

You appear in my vision
in those seconds when nerves tense,
mind becomes dense.

Your beautiful light brown eyes
sparkle with playfulness and life,
enlightening my darkest soul.

Though I am in doubt,
my heart still throbs.

I want you more than I had ever thought
I want you more than I had felt before
Filling this empty need with hued harmonies

I could forget about those flings
and goodbyes
if one day you decided to be in this

I wonder what you have been doing
I did not hear from you for months
You always appear in my mind
whenever I think of her

I still live with hope

infinity

January 14, 2014

You asked me out after months. I invited you to hang out and stay with me here for the night instead, even though I planned to be by myself.

You came, and I could see your hesitation and worries. Then, I told you, don't worry, I will not do anything with you.

Later that night, when we lay on the bed, you placed a pillow between us.

I was glad that I was not feeling well that night because I did not have anything to share with you.

Our night there was a secret. I do not want anyone to know who I am or why you are there.

Your perfume dazes my sleeping soul.

Has anyone ever told you how you
can make them have sleepless nights?

are you my fantasy?
September 2, 2014

Delicate kisses on your soft pink lips.
Cuddling through the night like our life
depends on each other.

Your slender legs cling to mine.
Embracing each other while watching
your favourite TV shows

Nestling our minds and heartbeats into one.

this is the reality

September 2, 2014

I was not expecting you to be at our friend's place today. I remember you told me you dislike celebrating festivities.

Whenever we are together with our friends, our interactions are awkward.

When you are by my side, every time you move closer to me, I lose the rhythm of my heartbeats.

Your fingers accidentally touch my knee while mine touches yours. You deflect. Then, seconds later, you move your knee and let it grace mine.

I overheard you were talking with our friend about your upcoming special day with someone.

My imagination is a dream, and
in an instant, it falls from its peak.

And so, you ended this abruptly.

There goes everything. Me standing
here by myself with no guts to spill it
all to anyone, especially you.

I was afraid to lose you as a friend,
and now I have lost both.

D D D
DCC D CA DEE
E E E DED
ED E DCEF GFED
D D D C DC
DCE DC

D D D C D C C D C A D E E
E E E E D E D
E D E D C E F G F E D
D D D D C D C
D C E D C

I have not been penning my thoughts for months,
oh wait, years.

another lie between friends

Jan 14, 2017

When I say I miss you, what I mean is that I would like you by my side.

When I avoid looking into your eyes, it means I am worried that you will haunt my days and nights again.

When I told you those chocolates and fruit tarts were delicious, I did not mean it. I have tasted better ones.

I love to see how proud you are, pleased with your choices.

These are lies between friends.

When your knees kept hitting mine several times under the table, I could not understand what you needed.

Frankly, I do not want to know whether you did not like mine touching yours. I just wanted mine entangled with yours.

This is just another lie between friends.

When you would not look at me most of the time when we used to hang out, I asked myself if there was something wrong. But not this time. I am not interested in knowing all the whys.

I would want to pay attention to what you look like now. Just so, it will last forever in my mind when you leave again.

Another lie between friends.

I could walk straight, I could balance myself, I could also walk at the other side of the road. But not tonight. I just want to be by your side, pretending just so I can hold your elbow and arms whenever I want to.

Touching your little boy's hand while he was asleep, just so I could feel the warmth of your body against my cold fingers.

When I ask about you and your family, my concern is only that you leave him out of our conversations. I will never ask about him.

When I tell you that you will have a happy life with him, it is another lie between friends.

We left you behind. I heard you whispering, like pleading behind me.

I gave up my egotistical view of the possibilities of why you disappeared these past years. I turned to you, held your back and let you walk ahead instead.

My core throbs
Thinking of that moment.

I don't understand why you kept complaining about what you looked like, and how you lacked this and that.

Is it because there is no one who told you how perfectly fit you are? I longed for those curves and your silky long hair. You flaunted your slender long legs at me every time we met and in text messages.

I hope one day you will realise you are exquisitely fine. Your beauty and how you dress yourself are two reasons I used to write about you.

September 30, 2017

The gem on your finger might have stopped me from telling you these unexplainable thoughts that I have every time I am alone in the darkness of my nights and early mornings.

purple stripes fading white

September 30, 2017

It is a perfect tint
highlighting your chin and
emphasizing your cheekbones

Fading white, purple stripes

Lit off the neon blue sky
shading our silent needs

September 30, 2017

In the minute our friends were careless,
I stole every second to look at you,
admiring every part of you under this scorching sun.
You light that darkness in the core of my heart.

If you ask,
still, I will reply yes
a thousand times.

strength

September 30, 2017

You said you made the scripture of art tattooed on the back of your neck to remind you of those days. Those days when you had to live life independently, determined and strong.

Tracing your scripture,
placing light kisses on every inch of it.

September 30, 2017

I don't know what it was.
Every time we were behind our friends,
I would hold your fingertips,
Intertwining our fingers
and locking our arms into one.

And to my surprise,
you let it be.

October 1, 2017

I refused to listen to anything or know anything about how you knew him. The evil side of me responded to our friend's remarks in a way to hurt you. And it worked out well.

October 8, 2017

Our arms were sweaty when we made contact. Instead of wiping it off like I normally did with others, we ended up staring into each other's brown eyes.

In my mind, my spiralling imagination let the evening breeze dry it off.

I cannot feel the electrifying physical response that poets describe, but I can feel that my heart no longer beats.

October 19, 2017

You noticed I was struggling with thirst. So, you handed me your tumbler after offering it to me twice that day. I was dehydrated this time, so I caved in. After me, your little boy, and then you.

I feel like I am part of both of you.

I am asking you this question.

Why did you acknowledge my existence only when you were with someone?

Nov 13, 2017

I numb myself by hustling through my days with works and
goals. Still trying. Today, my mind is filled with you again.
I check out your social media status and text messages.

Apparently, this is not over yet.
Engraved, embedded –
it has been three years.
You never leave my mind in the first place.

That throb, heart and all –
camouflaging the ticks of time.
All day today I have been thinking of you.

Needing you to be mine.

Nov 13, 2017

These familiar tunes remind me of our times together.
They constrict my mind and heartbeat, missing every
part of you.

Yearning for your touch.
Craving your attention.

Jan 11, 2018

Your voice is the soundtrack of my days,
harmonising with pride.
Calm, yet bothering my nights.

Jan 15, 2018

The numerical science of our stars
mingle with our illusions,
a whirlwind of our fancies.

Our paths collide again.

is it you or is it me?
June 12, 2018

I am fascinated by how destiny works.
Sometimes, when we look forward to it,
nothing works. Instead, it mercilessly
drifts away from us.

And when we are ready to let it go,
dispassionately with pride, it comes back to us.

Every time you said something,
you made me beam with hope.

You told me, "Tell mummy this is good".
Why?
You can say, "Tell your mum this is good".

Are you feeling the same way I do?

The anticipation of when we meet again,
even though your status forbids it all.

June 12, 2018

We met a few days ago. I could not concentrate on anything you were saying. Stereo emptiness.

That long warm hug when you wouldn't let go means a lot to me—that we both want it to be. So, I touched your face and held your hips intimately. I want you to remember every bit of it even though this is brief.

I had imagined we would do more than that. Honestly, while writing this, the image of you, your eyes and your genuine smiles, the warmth you made me feel when you kept your body close to mine, and at times when you act so cold, it makes me throb.

Veins of uncertainty have always been clouding my thoughts. And this time I will say yes if you ask me without asking myself anymore why I feel this way.

The droplets of rain on this train window are like a mirage of you drenched in a storm, seconds before I sleep every night and when I open my eyes.

I have no intention to deny your presence this time.
Will you give yourself a chance?

Silently, I refuse to back off this time,
even after what you told me that day indirectly.

You started it first, we will see what happens.
I might be hurt again, or this time it will work.

Whatever the outcome is,
our crossroads of thoughts,
our crossroads of walks.

Those times we were too close to be just *how friends are*.
Those intimate glances to be just *how friends are*.
Those that meant nothing to you meant the world to me.

I will not avoid or question myself or the universe this time—
 all the whys and hows.

This time I will risk myself.

Minutes of breath.

Holding it is like muting the orchestra
till when it will last.

Every stolen second,
it will be clearer than before,
fitting us all perfectly.

Mine throbs
I pulled you closer
Our chests beat in tune
As fast as the sound of lights

I could feel your long slender legs slipped between mine
You brought your lips near mine, hesitating

I could feel the intense air in between that small gap we shared
I touched your lower lips trembling with need and doubt

By the time I moved my fingers down to your neck
You closed the gap between us
Your lips touched mine
Yours desperately requesting entrance into mine

I have lost the rhythm
I have never felt this way
Your hands started to glide below my waist

And then you said
This is what you want, isn't it?

I know everything about us is not possible.

The air of autumn
as cold as the cotton in December
has always been like this.

A beginning without an end,
the end which you and I bent.

Sitting here at the edge of the globe,
frozen ice beneath my feet,
imagining you with your new life.

Wondering whether this is the life you dreamt of.
Never occurred to me to ask more about you.
What are your dreams?
What makes you happy?

It took a lot of courage to accept that I had lost you.

This is the moment you build your new chapter.

I guess you are only a dream of mine –
my inspiration.
I wonder why?

Could it be those features?
Crystallising reflections of these cafe windows,
charming the men,
captivating innocent women with wild hearts.

Those glances would make anyone wonder what you have
been thinking. The moment you smile, leaving those dimples
and starry brown eyes, I could not get you out of my mind.

If there are no limits,
I will choose you.

I have been wanting to do this all night.
Your territory,
hidden beneath the table
away from our friends.

Are you inviting me?

I gave you a glance,
as I could not move my eyes away from those slender ones.

I feel that you look forward for my touch
As you had rhythmically hit your knees with mine.

You were trying to tell me something, weren't you?

Seven years later,
I am back to square one.

It has always been you,
hasn't it?

Nov 17, 2019

Your relationship with someone who loves you—
The achievements of my dreams and goals.

The only difference is I can now accept who I am,
thinking that it will open me to new beginnings.

In the end, I came back to you.

It has been you all this while.

In fact, it is more blatant and intense than it was before.

I have been asking myself if it is because I have finally acknowledged who I am.

Why did you press your body into mine at the bar?
Why did you ask me to dance with you?

Why did you tell me to do whatever I want on the dance floor? Why did you flash your beautiful brown eyes and that smile at me?

Those are my weaknesses whenever I am with you.

You knew. You might have already known this since the beginning.

You told me how you actually felt before. I should be furious with you right now as I write this, but I know I have no rights. Because once again, I feel like this will go nowhere.

I can do whatever I want right now, but those lines which have become blurry for me might not be for you.

Whatever you have done to me might be just how you treated your friends. I could shed tears at this moment like I am about to, but I remind myself once again that I might have misinterpreted this.

It is you again that let me out of this same misery when I kept falling for anyone.

It is you again who could make me forget everything, like how you did six years ago.

December 30, 2019

Funny isn't it? Six years later I am back to this page, still writing pages about that one person. That one person who always inspires me to write.

Six years of many things that have happened to me. I have achieved my goals: earning a master's, travelling to places of my dreams, bridging new friendships and relationships, and all the ups and downs.

Six years of many things that have happened to you. Your relationship and those dreams of yours came true, bridging new friendships and relationships, and all your ups and downs.

You tied the knot about four years ago. A revelation that disappoints. If someone I was attracted had decided to live her own life with someone else, it would not affect me in any way, but your decision did.

These past years, I could put on a poker face whenever our friends mentioned your name. With distractions, I managed to piece myself together. Meeting new people, men or women, even though no one made me feel the same way. Whenever I saw that you had posted pictures with him, I could cope. It worked and has been for the past years—

And then something happens.

Those moments at the clubs, the rooftop bar and the dance floor changed everything. You knew which team I was since the beginning, and so you knew my weaknesses.

That one night of fun when we were intoxicated. You came to me at the bar while I was texting someone, that someone who was still sending texts that said, *I miss you* and *I wish you were here*. That someone who I needed to distract myself with.

You came to me at the bar, pressed yourself into me while glancing at my mobile phone. You did not even care about our friends who were observing us.

We talked. No, you talked, and I wasn't interested.

When our friends left for the dance floor, I took the opportunity to distract myself by listening to you. But I couldn't. Instead, I was memorizing the curve of your lips, trying to recall every inch of them, is if it was the same as before. Closer. Bolder.

While you were talking, intentionally, I glanced at your lips. When you looked at me, I quickly diverted my eyes, as if I did not want you to notice. I was intoxicated, but I could think.

You kept the conversation going, explaining incoherently something about dancing. And this time, you looked everywhere but at me. So, I took the opportunity to stare at your lips. This time, I guess I was wrong when I said I wasn't intoxicated.

After a while, you stopped talking and closed your eyes. Do not ask me why I didn't do anything. The only move I had the courage to make was to tuck your hair behind your ear a few times.

It has always been me who has these feeling for you. I am sure of my feelings but not yours. You have been avoiding me before you tied the knot.

I am not going to be the one leaving heartbroken again in this game of cat and mouse.

The only difference this time is I do not stop myself from expressing my feelings to you.

I am aware that I am bolder in the way I treated you—stealing glances and not worried if our friends noticed it.

You asked me whether I wanted to dance with you with those eyes. I had never seen you look at me like that before.

We held hands tightly on the way to the dance floor, ignoring the looks made by our friends. You asked me softly whether I would like to go into the crowd, and I replied, "Yes, I do". I wanted to be away from the prying eyes of our friends, just us hidden in the darkness. I wanted to be intoxicated only with you.

You brought me to a corner nearer to the DJ booth. My heart stopped when you pulled me hard, pressed into the back of your body. I could hear myself whimpering. You held my left hand and slid it up to caress the left part of your body, nearly touching your left breast. But at that moment, you let my hand go, so I was not sure. I was only courageous enough to slide my hand below your breast and let one of my fingers caress the lower part of where you needed me to.

As we walked farther into the crowd, you told me I could do whatever I wanted, so I held you close. I held you so close that if we moved an inch, this book of letters would not have ended like this.

My heart was beating like how I danced—without rhythm. You taught me how to dance. Whenever you said I could do whatever I wanted for the one hundredth time that night, I just held on to your waist or pulled you closer to me to make sure that I did not kiss you. I could not read your needs or wants from what you said.

But if it had been just the two of us, I would have let you do anything you wanted me to. Like how I am yearning for your touch at this moment.

There were two instances that have never changed in the last seven years ago: When you were still talking about your ex-boyfriend and when you let my hand go when you saw your friend who hadn't even noticed you.

to myself
Jan 4, 2020

Never have I ever learnt from my experiences. Never learnt from those days that I had to suffer and stay awake to get rid of this same person out of my mind.

These distractions to keep fit are one way I have tried to rid her from my memories. But then I am using her again, *her* as in the one and only true to my heart to help me to do so. I have succeeded all this while eliminating her from my mind that filled my nights and days. But how long can I live with this?

She helped me previously to rid them from my heart and anyone else after. I used her, but who do I have to use to forget her again?

What makes me think that someone who is already with the love of her life would want to spend her time with me?

With these uncertainties, is it me who is not interested in commitments? What if all this is not about building a relationship? What if it is about the person whom I am falling in love with?

the signs

September 13, 2020

When my heart aches in pain,
even a comedy doesn't heal any of it.

Those two signs, and that is it.

Shattering my heart into pieces.

the second avoidance

September 13, 2020

Today I shed tears for the second time.

I had doubts about how I felt about you because the edited photo that you posted hurt me. I know it could be nothing, but it seems like you are embarrassed when you are with me. And then you are proud of our friend's achievement, but never mine. I kept thinking about whether you wanted to disregard me from your memories.

Tonight, my heart shrinks so much more than usual. I am still not good in handling this. Am I making the same mistake again? Allowing myself to feel for you again, lifting the barrier and my guard to let you in. And then feeling the same thing over and over again.

I should tell you frankly not to behave like this whenever you are with me. Not to lead me on. But then another part of me reminds me that you didn't do this in the first place. It is only me misreading everything.

I did not respond to your last text once I saw your story. I did the same as earlier this year.

I needed to sleep it off a number of times to neutralize this gut-biting feeling. It's the only solution I am good at.

I wish I could tell you exactly how I feel.
I wish I could tell you that you meant a lot to me.
I wish I could tell you to lay beside me every night.
I wish I could tell you that I need you by my side.

I wish I could tell you that I kept thinking about you
day and night.
I wish I could tell you that I need you to hold me tight.
I wish I could tell you not to tell me about your exes.
I wish I could tell you to pull me closer when we were
at the bar.

I wish I could tell you it is alright to accept yourself.
I wish I could tell you that I do not want to lose you again.
I wish I could tell you I miss every part of you.

I wish I could tell you to come with me to the places of my
dreams.
I wish I could tell you that I want to do more things than a
friend would.
I wish I could tell you that I would like to do more than dance
with you.
I wish I could ask you whether you feel the same way as I do
whenever you are with me.

September 18, 2020

You asked,
if any of my dreams had not been fulfilled yet.

I replied in a tiny voice,
that not every dream of mine.
I continued softly because I am a coward.

I wish I could tell you that one of my yet to be fulfilled
dreams is to be with you. To be someone special in your
life, more than a best friend.

September 18, 2020

You said you have never kissed or even held hands with your exes. But you were fine when I held yours?

September 18, 2020

Today, you spontaneously invited me to come to your house for dinner when he was away for work. Do you know how much this meant to me? I have always given my time to you. I used to tell my friends not to ask me out at the last hour, but you have been the exception.

I am not sure whether these were the triggers to your invite. You asked me via text what I was doing over the weekend. I replied with, "I will be going to my friend's house for lunch." Specifically, I referred to this friend as "her".

Then, you talked about how I was now my own boss, and you felt like you were a nobody to me. However, I responded without overthinking, "You have always been my favourite". Apart from that, I told you that "I thought I am already obvious whenever I am with you, and you can still tell me those." You changed the subject.

Out of nowhere, your next text was an invite to your house. Me, alone. And of course, that eliminated all my assumptions regarding why you had invited me to lunch that day. How I am so restless thinking about how you might have fallen for our friend. You have done this several times since years ago. Those were my favourite times with you, when it was just the two of us.

We talked and talked. The things that we shared, including mine, were things we had never shared with our friends. I was comfortable talking to you because you have always been that person who is not afraid to come close to me with respect and caution. Oh, our friends do too. My friends do too. It is just that it is you. You have always been that special someone.

You shared stories comfortably, and then you said please do not tell our friends. I replied that I have never told them we went out together seven years ago.

You also said that you did not expect to share these things with me. Well, I needed to humour you for a moment by saying that I had used my charm. But then, I looked away. I could see how you laughed from the corner of my eyes. That shy laugh. I had seen it twice that night.

It was 11pm, then 12.30am. It was late, but I did not want to leave. You told me it was still early. And so, I stayed.

You still talked about your exes with me. Same as years ago. Only this time, I managed to handle the way I felt about your confessions more maturely. Especially after you told me about how you had to go through complicated situations all these years.

When you told me about your first ex whom you did not hold hands with, I knew why you would never make any moves when we were intoxicated while dancing. You told me that you were not the type who kisses and sleeps around. Well, I did not expect that from you. But you don't seem to be the type who never kisses and hold hands with your boyfriends. Babe, I have no idea why you are telling me these things when probably you could guess how I feel towards you. But this is the same type of conversation I had with other women. Their boyfriends, their ex-boyfriends. Actually, I am fine with it now. These mean nothing to me.

I slipped out several times during our chat. Especially after 12am. I felt so free talking about myself after this time. And I was honest to you when I told you that I was actually intoxicated and couldn't control myself when I was with you that night at the rooftop bar. Even though many times I told you I was fine. However, I did confess that I was afraid to lose control. And you asked me why. I replied with "I am so worried I will do or say something which I could not control in front of our friends". If you would like to know why, I was actually worried that I would kiss you in front of them. I did kiss your shoulder, babe, and if I continued, who knows what will be next. And I wanted to do more than that, but immediately my senses came back when I noticed our friend was taking a video of us. You had that smile again.

That night was one of my best nights. I had not felt like that in a long time – talking with someone who listens and who also shares their personal life freely and trusting me to hold on to it. Except for my love life, I was comfortable sharing with you. I wanted to share with you about my love life, or you could say relationships. But the thing is, babe, talking about it would lead to the part I am not interested in—the men I went out with. And that would lead to the next part of the story which I am not sure whether I can tell you about when I am sober.

We talked till 1.30am. I have never done this with anyone. In the past seven years, you were the only person whom I do not mind sacrificing my sleep and time for till early morning.

And, babe, that night was also when I could acknowledge your husband as someone you chose to be with. Since you told me about that challenge, trusting me with this information which your husband does not know, the only thing in my mind is for you to be happy and safe. In an instant, I put aside my ego, selfishness and doubts.

I asked you whether you loved your family and if this was the life that you wanted. And when you said yes, I let my guard down and told myself to acknowledge that you were with him. The only thing that came into my mind at that moment was that I do not want to lose you.

I want you to know that I will be there if you need me. I want you to know that I do not care if I might get hurt again by not telling you about this overwhelming feeling, and whether this is merely a one-sided story of mine, that you are not interested in me, or even if you prefer our friend instead.

What I am sure of after that night is that I want to be there for you. I want you to be in my life. Your presence makes mine bloom. I look forward to every moment with you. That is why I could behave the way I did throughout that night.

You have been my inspiration, and imagining my life without you is something I cannot accept. I am not looking forward to shedding tears and missing your kind smile, your dimples, your eyes, your hair, your touch, and the attention you always gave me. I look forward to always meeting you. It doesn't matter if we are with friends or just the two of us. I look forward to every moments with you, I want to see you flash that beautiful smile and sometimes those shy ones, laughing wildly with your playful antics. I want you to hold my hand or let me find yours in the darkness and hold it as long as I want to.

The heart of this is that you are there in my life whether you talk to me or not—it will not matter anymore. I just want to know you are there, happy with whoever you have chosen to be with.

September 20, 2020

I decided to put aside these feelings of mine, that egoistical need for you as long as you are safe and sound.

I don't know how to forget about these feelings towards you anymore. All day and night you never leave my mind. This time I had been trying, but you came back. Even so, my subconscious never wanted you to leave.

The difference between you and them is that thinking of you makes me throb with want, needing you all the time. Those fingers holding mine, thirsty for my touches.

And now, even though I know who you have been with and your vulnerabilities, I did not think of backing off like I always did before. In fact, I tried to but then decided not to. Probably, I am imagining all these, but part of me is telling me not to give up this time. I want to be with you more than before. I need you more than before.

I don't want to lose you again.

"I don't want to lose you again." I whispered in your ear, accompanied by the sounds of chatters and the live band. I looked into your brown eyes. Close enough that whatever I have imagined and wanted to do with you for a long time will be a reality.

You stood so close to me, close enough that my back could feel every part of your front.

I could have flirted a hundred times with you that night, winning in this game of cat and mouse. But you would have won the crown with merely one move because of your curiosity about what was on my phone.

Apparently, it seems like I am the bad girl in this relationship.

You are the one and only person who could have made me go back to my home late that night.

At 2am, I still don't feel the need to go to sleep.

At 5am, my diary is filled with the time we were together throughout the day, describing every detail when I was with you. Explaining the possibilities—the bits and pieces that I observed from the corner of my eye. Anything that I could catch a glimpse of when I was with you.

We just met two days ago. Five hours together, just us.
And now, I already miss you.

I decided to be at the party you had set up for our friend on 25 Sept.

I decided to not find reasons not to attend it and the night cycling on 9 Oct.

I decided to get rid of my petty jealousy after you invited me to dinner at your place. It was as if you could understand what I was going through.

September 23, 2020

I cannot get you out of my mind, probably because I do not want to. While I am working on my daily routine, you keep emerging in the vision of my mind.

None of the pages of this book I am reading right now is funny, but I cannot stop myself from smiling. I remember those times, and when we were together last Friday. I cannot wait to see you this weekend though. My heart is beating carelessly missing your presence. I cannot believe that I need you more than before, hurting the core of my being.

You said you made me a fried rice paste after you asked me about my favourite food. I told you, I cannot wait to see you this Friday, and in fact, I hope that I can meet you today, on my birthday. I am already deep into whatever this is, once again.

By the way, you posted a picture of us on the rooftop bar and cropped out our friend. You have made me happy. I know it is evil. For such a long time, I wanted you to acknowledge me with you. You cut it the way I had framed it on my bedroom wall. One of our friends asked me, "Who did you cut out?" And I replied, "Definitely not you and you are safe". I don't think she finds it funny though.

I do not want to be that selfish person who takes you from someone else who loves you too.

Why do I have to do that when love is in abundance? But on the other hand, I am being petty with your attention towards her.

But I still want some of your midnights, early mornings and whenever we wish and need each other.

You are that missing piece.

September 28, 2020

I was visualizing that you will help me with my hoodie, and I will hold your hands during our train ride because I miss you a million seconds.

It was better than I had imagined. You were the one who seems to be fine with it all the time. I was thinking that it will be only for a moment. But we held each other's hand throughout the ride. It is like we need each other. Well, I did, desperately.

You hooked my hand with a finger of yours when at some point our fingers were not intertwined. Tightly. I could not ask for more than that. I want this to never end.

Do you remember when our bodies started to drift from our minds? You talked about your ex and showed a picture of him to our friend.

I had begun to ignore what you needed to say. I have no idea whether you did that on purpose. Because from the corner of my eye, I noticed that you had glanced at me right after and then looked away.

Babe, I had to control myself. Your interest in your ex does not interest me, and it has been annoying me lately.

So, I need to talk this out with someone else. I have no other choice but to vent to someone. I made you wonder who I was texting. I let our friends say it out loud – a secret lover or whoever they wanted to assume it was. You were quiet, and I want you to know I don't like where this is going.

When I texted that I love you, I meant it.
You replied the same.
But I am not sure whether it meant the
same.

October 2, 2020

I have been waiting for those moments. I have no idea how to tell you how I feel, or whether I ever will. The only way I could is through how I behave when I am with you.

I will let time tell you and me that there is something about us that needs no effort.

We will try to ignore and avoid it as much as possible.

our energy repelled
October 2, 2020

I miss you. That is the only thing that came to my mind in the past few days.

For the first time ever, I could not hold hands with this friend of mine whom you had asked for my address. Both of us are usually physically close. Holding hands comes naturally when we are together. It does not matter whether she is with her partner. But yesterday, I could not. We held hands, but I felt like mine could only do so for a few seconds. There is this energy that is repelling us. I could feel she noticed it too.

I gave it another chance at another moment, but the same thing happened. I had to let it go.

Is it because of you? Truly, this has never happened before.

Autumn 2019 in Canada.

That is when and where it all started and then ended. Now, a fearless new beginning is rising with shades of certainty.

We cannot keep running away from this. Well, if you haven't, I have been.

I have been running away from this all my life. I have been denying this feeling since I had affection for my best friend in high school. I had no idea. I could not accept it until I was with my new classmates and colleagues who questioned me brilliantly and said it was not a big deal.

I need seven years of longing, learning and accepting to come back to you.

October 10, 2020

I promise that I will not text you or call you. I promise that I will not ask you out.

I promise that I will not touch your hands or hold your hands, even though I yearn to do so. I promise that I will speak only about the good things and not hurt your feelings.

I promise that I will physically distance myself whenever I am with you. I promise to treat you as a friend and not more than that.

I promise that every action I take prioritizes what makes you happy instead of my interests and feelings. I promise that I will not come back to you now, a year later, seven years later or forever. I promise not to look away when you start talking about your ex-boyfriend and him.

I promise not to be jealous or feel hurt if you are closer with our friend, more comfortable with her or whenever you distance yourself from me.

I promise myself that I will hold back my tears or hurt whenever I feel like you do not want me to be by your side.

October 15, 2020

Today is, in fact, the sixth day I managed to control myself by not texting you or liking any of your stories. However, because our friend needs my help to settle this arrangement for your birthday celebration, I have to break my rules. For the past two days, I have had a strong feeling that you will want to back out from it. From what our friend texted me, it sounds as if you are not happy or suddenly feel uncomfortable. That is the one thing I do not want to happen because all this avoidance I had towards you is from me. Whatever I am feeling right now is again overwhelming, and I have no idea how to manage it yet.

I have not spoken to any of my close friends for years on the phone. You were the first time ever. And like I said and promised earlier, I will do anything to make sure that you are happy. I am so glad that you did not feel abandoned. You sounded alright, and the reasons were justifiable. I am so glad we got to talk a while ago for half an hour. You told me about your little boy's school issue, and all that made me happy to hear your voice again.

Then you asked me about the cycling route and kept asking me who I would be going with again and again. This made me feel important. Alright, once again I am not dissecting it too much, but I love it when you asked me the details, sounding as if you were worried or concerned. When you told me that you had intended to bring your boy and join me but then decided not to, it was way more special to me.

For the past week before sleeping, I have tried to visualize us both probably unhappy with each other, and you telling me that you don't feel the same way as I do.

But every time, the storyline ended with us together.

November 2, 2020

I want to tell you that the reason I did not text you or responded to any of your stories is, yes, it is because of you. You told the three of us how last week you decided not to commit to anyone whom you think might not be interested in being friends with you. And furthermore, you did not text me either for that whole week. I feel I am one of them, but I did not take it seriously with your assumption, maybe because my reason for doing so is more like my feelings are too deep for you. It is a positive thing instead of not wanting to be your friend.

I looked forward to you reading the birthday card after we all left. And I hope you know that I am behaving like this not because I am not interested to be your friend. I want to be with you badly in any way that we can, but it is so overwhelming that I have no idea what to do. Telling you this might affect our friendship which I would rather keep forever.

I want you to know this: I have no idea why I did not feel jealous when you cried upon receiving the gift from our friend. It is probably because I have already set my mind to not feeling anything towards you, or it was now all about you. I wanted to hold you, but it would have been too obvious. I know I cannot help myself from being protective towards you, but I also do not want it to be so blatant that we are affected by someone saying, "No, you cannot do that!" or "This is wrong".

I am not sure whether you noticed this, that our two friends realised what was going on since at the rooftop bar.

By the way, when you made the fried rice for me, it meant a lot to me especially when our friends' expressions changed. You made me feel special. This includes the coffee with almond milk, when you pointed at yourself too, meaning to say, "like mine". I enjoy having some things in common with you.

Before I left at the end of the day, I wanted to hug you. But part of me said that since you were not moving towards me, it was a good opportunity for me to stay away from you and not touch you.

When I walked away towards the door, without expecting it, you hugged me from behind and placed your chin on my shoulder. Of course, then I have to break my own rule when I hold your face.

You deserve to know how perfect you are, and these letters and poems contain all those unspoken words of mine to you. I want you to know I value the time whenever we are together.

If I can survive all these years without you,
I could bury all these and move on.

November 12, 2020

Today marks it all clearly. I have no idea how many times I have shed tears controlling and holding this in. It feels like decades.

You sent bubble teas to my office, and I started to sob. You knew something was wrong. I know you knew why I changed my tone immediately the day before. You tested me with a question this morning, and I thought you knew, but I was furious again.

Frankly, babe, I was fine and energetic while chatting with you the day before, but I just couldn't control myself once you started mentioning her name. This time I couldn't.

November 13, 2020

This is the ending of this book of letters to you, my dearest. By now you should have guessed how much you mean to me. I think there were so many signs, but I refused to accept it.

I analysed every touch, every moment and second, whenever we were together. I still have tears in my eyes since you took that photo with our friend at the beach. How close you allowed her to be near you. How close you allowed her to let her body press into yours when you literally moved away when I did this to you. It is like you do not want to be associated with me.

Yes, there were so many gestures which I had assumed and misinterpreted, but this is the edge of my patience. I tried to observe whenever you were with her. I guess you were proud of her. You always seemed like you preferred to shy away from me whenever the four of us were together.

I do not mind if you like her. It seems she likes you too with how proudly she would tell us about every time you shared things with each other. I accept it as long as you are happy. It is just that it hurt when I could not tell you, and I had to hope and fill my mind with everything about you.

First, that gem on your finger will forever be yours, and second, I couldn't force you to feel the same way as I do.

Today, I am not giving up. I feel like it is better not to pursue you to get your attention when you do not feel the same way.

This book was written because I couldn't tell you how I feel. I do not want to lose you as a friend or destroy the relationship you have with the other two. But for me, on the other hand, I will risk it for myself.

Most importantly is that you are now happy with your family. I have to let this go again because if not, I will feel like I did again in the middle of Thursday, yesterday and days before.

Seven years ago, I thought I could get rid of this incomprehensible feeling by avoiding you. I thought that after achieving all my dreams, meeting new people and being attracted to them, it would help to make this go away. But when you appeared again and again, I tried and I kept trying in many ways – it was like a tug of war within myself.

This time I am telling myself to let this go.

And so, I let you go.

Index

About the Author

S.Sulianah, a writer of words in prose and poetry. She loves to share her thoughts and inspire others to do what they love, as well as learn about their passions. Her writing is a reflection of her heart's desire to be part of this world. She inspires herself through her books and imaginations by sharing her life journey and experiences with her readers.

Sulianah believes that while we are heading towards our dream and purpose in life, we should also enjoy its journey. Being grateful and appreciative would build a solid foundation in our life.

Masterpiece In Your Heart's Series of Poetry is her other published poetry book.